Gil
tim
poem.
love Drumm x x x
June '97

THE
ORDINARY
HOUSE
OF
LOVE

Theo Dorgan

for dear Eliza,
swimming into the poems,
Theo.
Annaghmakerrig '92

·SALMON·

PUBLISHING

Acknowledgements are made to the editors of the
following publications in which these poems, or
versions of them, first appeared:

*Ambit, The Cork Review, Cyphers, Disarm, Dundalk Poetry
Anthology, Fortnight, The Great Book of Ireland, Hill Field,
The Irish Times, Living Landscape Anthology,
New Irish Writing (The Sunday Tribune),
1990 (USA), Orbis, Poetry Ireland Review,
Poetry Nottingham, Poets for Africa,
Quarryman, Rebel, Salmon, Stet, Theatre Ireland,
Thistledown (Poems for UNICEF), Triskel Poets 2*

A number of these poems appeared in a broadsheet,
Triskel Poets 1, with Thomas McCarthy.
A further selection in broadsheet, **Words...Pictures,**
was illustrated by Val Bogan.

*At The Lubyanka, "But This Is Most Irregular ...",
In The Metro, Moscow* and *The Thaw* were first published as
A Moscow Quartet (The Sweatshop Press, Dublin, 1989).

A number of poems have been broadcast on RTE radio, on BBC
Northern Ireland and on Denmarks Radio.

Print origination by Bedouin Enterprises
Cover photography by Amelia Stein
Cover design by The Graphiconies
Printed by Colour Books Ltd., Dublin
Bound by Kenny's Fine Binding, Galway

Produced with the financial assistance of
The Arts Council / An Chomhairle Ealaíon

ISBN 0 948339 51 9   Softcover £4.95
ISBN 0 948339 50 0   Hardcover £8.50

1990 Salmon Publishing, Bridge Mills, Galway.

To the memory of
my Father and my Mother

For there is no sea
it is all a dream
there is no sea
except in the tangle
of our minds;
the wine dark
sea of history
on which we all turn
turn and thresh
*   and disappear.*

John Montague

Contents

THE
ORDINARY
HOUSE
OF
LOVE

NIGHT OVER THE MOUNTAIN AND THE CITY

No rage in the hawthorns or in the State plantations,
Only the rain uneasy over Musheramore.
No tumbling of stone in mountain torrents,
Only the granite crumbling in the heather.
Here where she laughed in the face of the wind
Not a rabbit darts, not a cloud rolls along the ridge.

The lights on the barrack square are shrouded,
And the sentries at whose innocence we guessed
Are long gone from the nights of forgotten winter.
Now a car echoing in the empty street awakes no start,
Here where she'd toss her hair and wave up to the window,
As in so many places over the years, over the city.

So often in need of soothing, now she is soothed
Away forever into a long, untroubled sleep.
So often the ice-breaker on Christmas morning
On swims I could never dare, now she is swimming
Out into the dark, as briskly as she strode
Over the mountains — leaving us dumb to say

How much we loved her, each in our own way.
How a clear voice echoing in the street will turn our heads,
How a stone crumbling, or a stream rolling or a wave
Breaking, will speak of her to us forever.
Too many deaths have unmade my courage for anything
But the images I hold stubborn and unshakable in my heart.

i.m. Clare Barker

CLOSED CIRCUIT

The light of evening falls in swathes
Over the Northside and Blackpool.
Children are rolling downhill
In the long grasses of Bell's Field,
Over and over, elbows tucked tight,
Drenched in the smell of earth.
They never seem to hit rocks, or roll
In the signature of the city,
Broken glass.

Laughter and light trip memory inward,
Rooftops press forward
Some long-forgotten summer and I fall
In delicious vertigo into a classroom
Where I sit silent, staring ...
Even that youngest swallow, climbing
On leafsmoke, starting on the miraculous
Journey south, bends downwind for mountain home
Though he has never been there.

... I sat in the smell of wood and chalkdust
Baked in the sun with smell of the slaughterhouse,
My mind soaring through the roof, neckhairs bristling.
I hung for hours over familiar lanes and streets,
Picturing another home in another country.
The calls of my classmates after school
Were high, wide and shrill — familiar and alien,
The memory neither fades nor fails to haunt —
Afternoon music over North African streets.

And today I think you are a village in those mountains.
There are squares and fountains, wells of cool darkness

In the centre of each house, the walls soaked
In a whiteness that makes the heart ache; every house
Is a house of mystery, even the scrubbed tables are blessed
With the imprint of your daily use and habit.
Open the drab green shutters and lean out,
I have been flying to you since childhood, and I thirst
For the shock of your fountains, the cool shade of your care,
Let me roll like a child forever in your hair.

for Suzanne

A NOCTURNE FOR BLACKPOOL

Dolphins are coursing in the blue air outside the window
And the sparking stars are oxygen, bubbling to the moon.
At the end of the terrace, unicorns scuff asphalt,
One with her neck stretched on the cool roof of a car.

A key rasps in a latch, milk bottles click on a sill,
A truck heading for Mallow roars, changing gear on a hill.
The electric hum of the brewery whines, then drops in pitch —
Ground bass for the nocturne of Blackpool.

The ghost of Inspector Swanzy creeps down Hardwick Street,
MacCurtain turns down the counterpane of a bed he'll never
sleep in,
Unquiet murmurs scold from the blue-slate rooftops
The Death-Squad no-one had thought to guard against.

The young sunburned hurlers flex in their beds, dreaming of
glory,
Great deeds on the playing-fields, half-days from school,
While their slightly older sisters dream of men and pain,
An equation to be puzzled out again and again.

Walloo Dullea, melodious on the Commons Road, hums airs
from Trovatore,
The recipe as before, nobody stirs from sleep
And 'Puzzle the Judge', contented, pokes at ashes —
"There's many a lawyer here today could learn from this
man".

North Chapel, The Assumption, Farranferris and Blackpool,
The mass of the church in stone rears like rock from the sea
But the interlaced lanes flick with submarine life
Older than priests can, or want to, understand.

This woman believed Jack Lynch stood next to God, who
broke the Republic.
This man beyond, his face turned to the wall, stares at his
friend
Whose face will not cease from burning in the icy sea
—torpedoed off
Murmansk from a tanker. He shot him, now nightly he
watches him sink.

Here is a woman the wrong side of forty, sightless in her
kitchen
As she struggles to make sense of the redundancy notice,
Of her boorish son, just home, four years on the dole, foul-
mouthed,
Of her husband, who has aged ten years in as many days.

The bells of Shandon jolt like electricity through lovers
In a cold-water flat beneath the attic of a house in Hatton's
Alley,
The ghost of Frank O'Connor smiles on Fever Hospital Steps
As Mon boys go by, arguing about first pints of stout and Che
Guevara.

The unicorns of legend are the donkeys of childhood, nobody
Knows that better than we know it ourselves, but we know
also that
Dolphins are coursing through the blue air outside our
windows
And the sparking stars are oxygen, bubbling to the moon.

We are who we are and what we do. We study indifference in
a hard school
And in a hard time, but we keep the skill to make legend of
the ordinary.
We keep an eye to the slow clock of history in Blackpool —
Jesus himself, as they say around here, was born in a stable.

for Mick Hannigan

SWIMMING DOWN DEEP TO BEFORE TIME BEGAN

The night I sank into your troubled eyes
I was watching my words,
I was watching my step
While you were swimming deep into my heart,
Gently, disturbing nothing
As the soft rain hung fringes on the trees.

What depths we can sometimes reach,
In unremarkable talk,
In an ordinary caress
Sounding truths laid deeper than we know,
Gently, disturbing nothing
Like people who have been talking for centuries.

If I close my eyes I can feel my breath
As the pain eases out,
As the words ease out,
Hesitant, night-swimming fish;
Gently, disturbing nothing,
Sentences schooling to an unexpected thought:

In Lake Baikal there are boneless fish,
They melt in the shallows,
They melt in the air.
What lives they must lead there in the dark,
Gently, disturbing nothing,
Lives at an unexpected depth, like ours tonight.

THE MOTHERS, THE CHILDREN, THE LOVERS

Our Lady of Flowers is gone from
Your city and mine
The children stare vacant, the
Grip of their laughter is grim
The soot falls on streets where
You skipped in a loop of strong rope
There's a road through the gardens
Where once I robbed apples at night.

The bones of St. Valentine rest
Behind Whitefriars walls
And old love is bleeding to death
Where we once placed our trust
The trick is to dance beyond
Hopelessness and beyond hope
Your eyes on the inward dance
Where you may think to find me.

The bellnotes from Shandon fall
Silver and cold on Blackpool
And the ladies of Fatima pray
For their thin laughing kids
When I turn in your arms I can feel
The blue lightning start up
The redemption of childhood
The sword held aloft with the cup.

Somewhere your mother and mine
Are just starting to talk
In orchards they dreamed of
When young and it wasn't too late

For the dreams that they had of the love
That flares out in the dark
In the spell that they bless us for
Praying that our nerves can hold out.

for Paula Meehan

FLEDGLING

Ungainly biped
By a lurch in time
Tipped from the nest

Blinks the harsh light
From tender eyes and
Stumbles in long grass.

The green blades
Are piercing screams.
Massed trees lean over him
With a soft, terrible roaring,

His burgeoning wings mimic
The torsion of drowning
And under this panic
A dreamflash, seen in the egg —
Promise of owldark,
A moon fitfully glimpsed
Behind bare trees —
And this abruptly extinguished.

JOURNEY BY NIGHT

On the high road through the Gorges du Tarn
When the car bucked at a flat turn
And bowled at the edge
On a wedge of rubber screaming,
Even then, with the gates of panic breached
We did not break our silence of hours,
Our deep trust in the willed path.

And if I now say the depth of time touched us,
The sense of the great bowl we run down in a curve,
It is only to say what as a child I knew
— there is nowhere to fall
and speed can buttress will —
When you have somewhere to go you simply go.

ONE MORNING IN MAY

The grasses you walk in
Are freighted with dew,
Your coat flecked
With prismatic drops,
The crystalline rout
Of multiplied suns &
The song of the lark
Are focussed in you

Who should be crowned
With flowers and ivy,
Your high breasts bare
 Long hair cascading
Over your shoulders —

But what would the neighbours say
To your bright ankles glinting,
To the rippling of the reed-pipe,
To my faun's grin as I perch on the step
Of a battered Renault 4?

SUNDAY AFTERNOON

In the ordinary house of love
We move quietly from room to room.
Here you are pensive at a window,

Your cheek flat on the green pane,
And the oak outside marks
A corner of silence in a Summer room.
Beyond again, in a greater room,
Swallows curl to a punctured ceiling,
And beyond again ...

And all of my windows open to the fresh wind,
To the gold light refined through your hair.
A knock on the door of childhood

And the walls dissolve in music,
Soft beat of your dancer's foot,
White recession of doorways in your eye.

NEXT MORNING

Starting the engine you turn and smile,
At a button's touch blossom is wiped
To the corners of the windscreen,
Crushed fans that stubbornly endure
To my front gate.

Crush me a fistful for token of last night,
Cherryblossoms drifting at the window,
Your breasts nuzzling to my lips:
Your smile hints that you're determined
To forget.

ROBBING ORCHARDS

I love the parish of the lovers' bed
Where the turned-down corners of a sheet,
Stepping into a room at evening,
Tug at the memory like a half-forgotten street.

The hemmed edge lies at the foot of a wall
I might have climbed, belly warm with danger
Before dropping to the rich, wet grass,
Eyes glinting for the laden tree.

Savage delight then, to race dogs to the wall,
Scrambling by intuition to the top again
Before dropping to the warm pavement, grass stains
On my running-shoes, an apple rolling towards the kerb.

Sometimes you bite me as we fall over the wall
And afterwards I taste apple on my breath,
Absolute self in the sweat rolling down my chest,
Soaking forever the linen of a remembered street.

FOUR A.M.   JAZZ ON THE RADIO

Somebody cynical out there in the dark
Brushing the snare with a flick on the backbeat,
Midrange piano liquid and blue and the sax
Curling under, low; thinking of you.

There's a Forties feel to this,
Latenight streets and a single car
Far off in the distance, maybe rain
Sulky and cool somewhere close by.

Somebody moody is plucking a double bass
Like he was drumming on heartstrings,
In the wings, almost, a laidback angel
Popping the congas like he was slapping down hope.

Somebody wake that man on the sax,
Something a little up-tempo is called for here.
Something to get a little focus going
Before I light another cigarette.

Radio starlight in the early hours
Far from your bed and eyes.
Tell me, the piano man is asking,
How did a kid like you get to be so wise?

A Sudden Grasp Of Modigliani

Pungent dust beneath the umbrella pines,
The oily sea licking the smooth rocks.
More than a summer thunder in the air
Pressing our conversation down to silence.

And so we walk, together and apart
Untouched into the troubled afternoon,
Your rope-soled shoes a vivid aquamarine,
Scuffing the red dust as we talk of art

And children and the flowers of Provence,
Anything but the questions that hang fire
In the yellow clouds pressing from overhead.
The pines are dry as if already dead.

Like a thin thread of water underground
Urgently twitching, that the clouds should unburden
and let fall weight of salvation and grace,
My pulse goes through my breathing, snagging yours

Until a new rhythm slows time and our walk.
Your eyes are heavy-lidded when I turn to look
And a stray lock follows your cheekbone forward.
Perfection in mid-stride, an end to talk.

"BUT THIS IS MOST IRREGULAR ..."

In Pushkin's house on the Arbat we put on felt slippers,
To glide between two tours on a private visit.
We are here and not here, and the guides are at first
Uneasy. They hand us from room to room, like ambassadors
Or prisoners. I admire the tiled walls behind the stove,
The polished floors, the ceilings plain and low.

Portraits and first editions, pages of manuscript behind
Glass. Ornaments, polished windows, the poet's writing desk.
There are others before us, we hear their voices; others
Behind, heard but unseen. The guides ask urgent questions
Of my interpreter, casting me anxious glances, ill at ease.
I feel like the man himself, being processed towards the Tsar.

In primary school we had parquet floors like these, every
Christmas we'd fit socks over our shoes and glide in lines
From end to end in glorious misrule until the floors shone
Like polished apples. The impulse is irresistible — I start
Skating around John Field's old black piano and in a sudden
Crack of sun everything comes right. The guide's face

Breaks in a smile and she sheds her careworn years, Lena
Is grinning from ear to ear and another guide appears and
then
We are all four revolving in a slow ring, mayhem and
Giddiness in the poet's house at last. A horseman riding by
Would find us hard to resist, would surely refuse his destiny.
To be cast in bronze forever could never compare with this.

Come and lie long beside me one more time,
Long and slender beside me, through this quiet night,
Beyond passion or the body's ambition, merely tender
And cool, listening to the silence between heartbeats.

We'll have sheets of starched white linen
And heavy blankets to press us under
The surface into quiet deeper than sleep.
We'll have the blue October light
And keep each other awake with minute shifts in place,
Contact withdrawn at the ankle, renewed at the hip.

Tonight for the last time we'll let the moorings slip,
Pushing our lovers' boat away from the stone house
Under the elms, pushing them out into the lake
Of forgotten dreams, pushing them out and away
From us as they turn to each other under the stars with
A practised and complete ease, so sure of themselves ...

We'll have rest then that we never dreamed of
That first time and the many times since when
We slowly undressed in this room, hearing the silence
deepen.
We'll have rest as we watch them drift out into the dark,
Marking each wave-slap against wood with a caress,
Twining themselves in the rhythm of what is.

Bright stars winking in the clear month before winter.
We always knew, even when soaring into that first lift,
It would come on a night like this — the elms creaking

On the margins, lake slapping against stone, timbers settling
To the swell. Bodies reaching to surpass themselves.
An old, old story, unfolding on the ceiling.

Beyond heartbreak and joy, the silence between heartbeats.
After all our journeying and fret, this promised room.
Come and lie long beside me one more time,
Long and slender beside me through the quiet of this night.

FOUR THOUSAND SURVIVORS

The horse of the century trembles
Under the alder tipped with bronze,
Flanks of black silk raked by thorns.

He has made a long flight in terror,
Fleeing the sea of millions dead
To this place of water

Beneath tall cliffs, thicket of sun,
Swell of birdsong; his shadow creeps east
To his birthplace as evening ignites.

Rearing, his head among branches, he flails
The bright air, churning close turf, nostrils
Flung wide to the savour of earth

Then plunges to part the green waters;
Shouldering out, clattering on submerged rock,
White roar of the waterfall in his ears.

High on the cliffs the assembly lifts to depart.
Young men put on the wings of eagles,
Women already are treading air,
A clear bell-note fractures the horizon.

MORNING IN WINTER

Your eyelash rasping on my stubble
We puff breath at the window,
Through the clearing pane watch
Birds on crisp branches,
The city skyline emerging.

The long garden invites
That we step out,
To feel white grass crunch
Underfoot, heel slide over
Stalks wet under frost.

Soft shock on the window, snow
Funnelling through the tall elms.
We snap into waking
As loops of your laughter
Fall ringing on my ears,
We dress and fall out
Into a world made over, new.

WEDDING GUESTS ON THE ANNIVERSARY

They vanished in a flare of light and laughter,
The dark doorway torched by her dress and veil.
We could hear them crossing the hushed water-meadow,
 The car coughing into life, the roar dwindling.

Now we can hear a different car approach,
Ghost of a car's ghost tunnelling up the years,
We strain to the windows to imagine them,
The open door spilling light into the yard.

Time we were gone. We'll leave them to the wine
On the scrubbed deal table, the ticking clock
And all the talk they've gathered from the years.
No fear but they've plenty to look back on

And look forward to. We have other care,
Blessed if they grasp at the same luck as this pair.

for Marie and Seamus

BIRTHDAY

Red wine in white porcelain bowls,
Susan is having a birthday and
We are all invited.

Bread smells from the yellow kitchen,
Broad armfuls of corn, tied with red ribbon,
Hang from the rafters, baskets
Of fruit range along shelves

And there is music like crystal,
Music that strays from the raw hills,
Music of many voices, tangled
In easy conversation.

Bushels of flowers are heaped in the windows,
Ripe yellow rushes carpet the floor —
Gathered by Nuala of the pale shoulders —
Each knock brings an old friend in from the door.

Red wine in white porcelain bowls,
Susan is having a birthday and
We are all invited.

SAVAGE

My love is a cat
And has me plagued with
Claws and scratches, feline
Insouciance and
Her habit of dropping
From lamp-posts and branches,
Battening on my scruff.

Sometimes she's nice
And brings me roses, dangling
From her slack jaw —
Fresh-cut, blood red roses.

KILMAINHAM, EASTER
to the memory of James Connolly

Blood and cold stone, rust
Thickening to a seam of crystal,
Stain on the jailyard
Paving we cannot lift.

Crash of the volley and our hope.
When they carried our your stretcher
The yard darkened to a well of shame
And steadily it grows darker.

This is the shrine our rulers keep
And today they have graced it with flowers.
Let us grant them at least their honesty,
Their naked love of prisons.

ALL SOULS' EVE

Deirid lucht léinn gur chloíte an galar an grá...
Nuair a théas sé fá'n chroí cha scaoiltear as é go brách.

Once a year in a troubled sleep
That room stands drenched in light
Where I sit and watch us both asleep
In a cold sweat of fright.

A high room where the boards creak
The skylight faced with frost
Our bodies interlaced in sleep
And the world long lost.
Beside the bed my blue jeans
Lie crumpled in your dress
Dawn light coming in as we
Unconsciously caress.

The germ of death is in that dream
There in our mingled breath
There in our silence and our speech
— as when you moan not yet.
We lie in the breath of lovers lost
To the world since time began
Their souls the patterns in the frost
As you turn beneath my hand.

Once a year in a troubled sleep
I watch until we wake
... this is a vigil that I keep
And never must forsake
Until slow bells break

From a world long lost
Sleep-drugged lovers
To a city gripped in frost.

There is no time and all time
As we surface to a kiss
What we were before we died
A game compared to this.
No world and a whole world
In an innocent caress
Never again the same world
We leave when we undress.

> *The learned men say that love*
> *Is a killing disease.*
> *When it goes to the heart*
> *It will never come out again.*

CATCHING THE EARLY MORNING TRAIN

Drowsy in perfumed sleep you turn and watch
As I rise in the cold air and dress,
Finding my things by touch in a gleam of streetlight.

Courage is needed to dress, courage to watch.
The gravity we can sometimes hold at bay
Is the real power at moments like this.

Isn't it strange?
We shift between what we claim and what claims us,
Neither free nor unfree, neither moving nor at rest.

Sharp wind off the river cuts your perfume,
A boat hoots mournfully, standing out to sea.
How hard it is to resume the you and me.

SONG: PREMONITION

Into my mind a ship came sailing,
In her hold you lay as dead,
At your feet white wolves were howling,
Seven bright candles were at your head.

On the bare oak deck lay a sheaf of barley,
Dolphins plunged in the foaming wake,
High astern hung glinting stormbirds,
Curls of ice in the vault of day.

I thought of the mountain on which we rambled
To view the landfall to Kenmare Bay,
I saw with the mind's eye that silver birchwood
Where drunk with love we often lay.

In the lane this morning a curl of woodsmoke
Called up your face in the winter air,
A dark foreboding was in your features,
A lightning-chaplet restrained your hair.

All the long day great winds are rising,
Salt lightning roars rock to shining clay,
A hawk erupts through the rainlashed window,
Bright talons gleaming in a burst of spray.

Oh where are you love, where do you lie,
What storm confounds you, homeward bound?
Send me a sign the line's not broken, that
Binds your heart to our home ground.

SHE INVITES

When unringed fingers move to weave
She ceases momently to breathe,
An old blues floats in to fill
The space departing dancers leave.

Her eyes flash
From inward focus, hips
Barely move, except when
Pelvic concaves shift
To trap stray notes.

Spare and select, her gestures
Grace the lean music, they pull time
And the lines of the room
To a tight, breathing cage.

Press of the music parts her lips,
Heel hammers a slow beat
As she swoops to greet me —
Black hair flaring, her arms held wide.

for S.A.

HER BODY

Becomes pure power
Sufficient to self
A form of light.

Sprayhead she fountains
In whirling of stars
Benefactress of galaxies
Axis of night, until
Brightcrown bows down
And she flares, turning, then
Dies to her root in damp earth.

Through slant fields of evening I am drawn
To learn my nature at her feet.

BLACK FOX WOOD

By Black Fox Wood I came
And stood an hour before your door.
By first light I had forgot
What I was waiting for.

In that wood there is a tree
Whose roots plait in a rushing stream.
As I returned again I met you
Waiting there for me.

We kissed, and I remembered what
I'd waited for an hour,
When I got to your house again
You were standing in the door.

We kissed, and stood in Black Fox Wood.
Embraced, and then instead
Of close turf and the wild thyme
We were sprawled across your bed.

And ever since it's all the one
To me, love, where we are —
Under the light of a paling moon
Or a dark and wayward star.

The bed became our marriage-bed
And each the other's good
Whether we're here on a city street
Or at large in Black Fox Wood.

At The Lubyanka

There are no queues today, Anna Akhmatova,
At the black gate of ice in Dzherzinskaya Square.
Last night a bride in a veil of lace
Walked hand in hand with her young man
Past the grim prison of eternal renown
Without a backward or a sideways glance,
The bell of her laughter antiphon to your Requiem.

Now that the terror has changed key,
Now that it drifts like ash, like
Funeral music through the veins of
The wide world, tell me
Where will the grief of mothers find
The point of its pure expression,
Where should we hope to find now a voice like yours?

INSOMNIAC

Her long arms encircle,
Will never hold me;
Whose hair on my pillow

Is honey-coloured
Even in moonlight,
Her sharp features
Blurred in sleep.

My friend is untouched
By winter's breath.
Her skin blooms to velvet
Soft to the touch.

Her necklace lies in a pool of wine,
It bruised my lips when she
Crushed me close, as her words
Still bruise my heart:

You who have not learned patience
Must first learn care, then
Come to trust who grips the knife
That cuts the lifeline to give life.

Floating after making love you are often
Oracular. Will it be you curled here beside me,
Burrowing your cold nose against my ribs,
Who will deliver me to death?

The Sea-Gypsy And Her Lover

He

I am the murmuring surf beneath the nocturne,
The shearwater piercing the wave arcade.
I am the wrist and gesture of the gypsy,
I am the wavearch and her figure in the arch,
I am the hair falling across her face
And the clear stars drizzling through her hair.
My breath is the far-off murmur of the surf
And my true songs are nocturnes.

She

Turning and building back always on my heart
I am the oldest port you ever sailed for,
Mine in the dog-watch is the unseen hand
That pulls the helm over into the belly of a wave,
Mine and mine only the brief skyward path
Climbing the silver inside of the uproll when the moon spins
And the heart screams inward home, home —

I am the music then,
I am the clash of bracelets and the space hung
Where the seabird was,
Mindless and cold like the murmuring of the surf,
Nailed for all time to the crossmast of your bones.

EYE OF THE STORM

i)
Drumrolls on the windowpane,
Forked lightning over the terraced
City where I find myself again.

ii)
High in your room we float, caught
Up in play of star and planet,
Feeling the pulse of common orbit.

iii)
Each cell of me swells
To your lunar being,
We rise up
And overflow
The well-walled earth.

iv)
Limitless, the lid-pictures
Of selves beyond skin

Silence beyond the bloodveil
Hiss in the ear fading

Rain coming downhill among trees

REVENANT

Pale gleam of her hips
As she swings by.
Black fall of her hair
Brushes her shadow on the wall.
  smell of woodsmoke as I rise and follow

Alder taps on the windowpane,
Leafshadow flickering
On a harpsichord.
Fingers of ivory drift

Out over the black keys
As she hunches to begin.
But instead she turns,
Unhoods her eyes for me.
  smell of jasmine, nettles, earth after summer rain.

for Pauline

COMING EVENTS

Consider the ghostlines feeding the piper,
His face draining to mask of stone,
The liquid death in his music, look

How he coaxes a last grace from the space
Between stars, how his wrists battle the chanter...
Come set your foot to the green lament.
We are but shadows fixed in flesh,
This earth a greeting-place.

NASTY ARCHER

You are more fragile than you were
Loving me more than you did before
Love's bite struck bone. Look at him
Smile, nasty archer at his mischief.

Fragility is strength, we know the paradox.
The question in your eyes, which mirrors mine, is
What, when we walked here first and had not
Certainty of love, made both hearts beat one beat?

In The Metro, Moscow

No buskers at the gate,
The only time I have ever gone
Underground without music.
No advertisements on the wall,
Nothing to speak of the world,
To tempt us back.
Bronze of Pushkin, polished
And serene; overhead planes
Of the Thirties,
A parachutist descending.

The first stage is easy
But at the interchange
I hesitate, spelling
The letters of an unfamiliar tongue.
A woman my mother's age approaches,
Examines the card on which I have
Carefully written down my destination.
Gripping my elbow she sets off
Through the labyrinth. I tell her
My nation, she is amused, indifferent.

I am borne along under warm arrest.
We cross corridors, climb stairs,
Descend again, turn corners,
Eventually we arrive. Meanwhile
Her daughter is embarrassed, furious.
I shake hands with the mother but
I am looking at the daughter.
Her face is a mask of insolent stone,
Clamped in stereo headphones.
I wonder what journey I have interrupted.

ALMOST

Stooping at night to shield a match
From the street wind, or stopping
To watch the dust lift from
The cracks between paving stones,
I see your feet pick crisp steps into the afternoon,
A small pain twisted into your shoulders.

A moment neither accepted nor refused.
Though the match flares and goes out,
Though the dust hangs in my eye,
I remain hunched, trapped in the dream
Of your small feet walking away,
The look in your eye before you turned.

for Thomas and Catherine

FALLING SOUTH

It might be a prairie scene from the American midwest,
A ruined farmhouse in a dry, ploughed field, the melancholy
Burned out of it by the high Beltane sun
The outlandish voices around me falling silent.

Rocked on the evening train I gather images
Select, discard, the eye seduced by what's thrown up
At random, the ear tuned to Dido's last great aria
How the thing surfaces from what is random.

It might be a wood I plunged in as a child after school,
Released to the mysteries of the grove by an act of will,
This copse spinning quickly from the corner of vision
The world might be random, selection never is.

The day comes when the heart tires of continual rejection,
Tires of the endless effort to hold to the mooring chain,
And the mind invests its intelligence in the senses
*Sun on my hand, the deserted farmhouse, trees in their
stillness*

In every trip that I make there is a voice speaking,
I drift in my seat, straining to catch the wavelength,
To make something coherent in the space between cities
But it falls away in a reverie of your highflown hands.

The sun drifts high against evening cottage walls,
I imagine the silence we might make there before night
Comes in but I cannot imagine this as a coherent life
Falling away to the south in sensual freefall.

ATAVIST

I am a flame crossing the river
Rain is hissing on the water
I do not waver but incline
Against the vector of my passage
Fin of some great seagoing fish.

And though this bridge
Husband its carriageway
To a ribbed vaulting aisle
I am crossing a whale-road
Under arch of bleached bone,
The flame that I am
On this dark night at your window
Burned before Christ.

Statement Of The Political Exiles

If it takes anger, we will be angry.
If it takes cunning, very well,
We will be cunning.
If it takes patience we will be rock
Stubborn in the stream.
If it means forced marches
In the dead of the night,
Look for us when the moon is down,
One foot steady after the other.

If it means prison,
Bind our wrists, take us.
If it means beatings
We will break like reeds,
Like reeds we will spring back
After the storm has gone over.

We can be silent in the airports,
Our songs locked in our hearts.
We can be faceless
In your cities,
Anonymous in your fields;
We can dissolve like salt
In the sea of tears,
We can be sand
Drifting at the margins.

If it takes all the aeons needed
To crush carbon into diamond,
Hear us:
Those rivers run in our blood,
That garden was promised us
Before time began.

Who owns the light?
Who has charge of the air?
If it takes anger
We will be angry but
In any case, believe us:
We are surely going home.
Can you make a bird
Fly backwards?
Believe us, we are going to our home.

for Kader & Louise Asmal

Dr. Hoffman's Discovery

The lichen blooms
Into light and strikes,
Curled edges already
Beyond the forehead,
Skirmishing inward
To the brain's light.

The brain's light,
Determined
To sell itself dearly.

On a day in summer over Ballingeary
Walking the hills with nothing in mind
I stopped too long by a glowing rock
And lost my reason to the god of war.

A stone will do it,
A drop of water
At a leaf's tip,
Will trip your defence
And feed you to the world.

Mars is a sponge for light,
A god of harvest;
In the brute swing of his arc
Your light has perfect value, perfect weight.

WOMAN IN FOREST

I imagine you rising from a dark pool
Late sun, early moon silvering your black hair.
A still pool, and the forest musk
Rank in the ferndust where I lie.

Late evening, then, when all the creatures
Are watchful and at rest.
You reach for your cheekbone with your palm,
Considering the reflection of yourself.

All my attention's on the slow fall
Of water through your hair; your eyes
Are agates there, I'll rue the day
They fix on me in judgement.

Meanwhile, like any fox or rabbit,
I drink in the evening air,
Lap at your waist as you rise up,
Gambling with my whole future in your stare.

DAY OF RECKONING

i)
Harpnotes like motes in the clear air
Skylight tipped high to morning

Sunlight in bars on your tawny flank
Soft cheek muting the strings

How many nights under sheets of lead
For this plangent, parting air?

ii)
Framed in a blue door you mouth bubbles of gold
And your hand bobs in an underwater salute

My ear is a tall sail
Tilting toward your blessing

Time boils in my veins,
I shrug and displace myself.

iii)
In the full glare of noon
White waves on a white beach

Swallows in panic stitching the wound
Seathistles leaching to acid green

Sweat starts to my bleached palms,
Dull presentiment pounds in the blood.

iv)
Climb inland. Far beneath, a deep pool —
And down dives an arrow-arc of water.

Blue translucent deer
Ricochet off the wall of my look

My love is a drowned white city,
Submarine light gilding her evening towers.
v)
Quartz leaps from the hammer blow
In the waning light

Repetitive echoes map valleys of dusk
A heron fades down the river's fall

A worker is quarrying stars,
Stars fountaining in his face.

vi)
On the high plantation road
A fox comes careless of noise

A wheel coming up through bracken
A fox careless of noise

We stitch the wound with a look
Silent regarding silent.

vii)
The wind stirs in the pinetops and
The dark is climbing towards me from the sea.
Here I pick up my solitary way.

Starring the gulf between us,
The cottage lights flick on.
I cannot tell which of them now is yours.

> *Star of the valleys,*
> *Star of earth,*
> *Star that was counted*
> *And is now lost.*

CARNIVAL

Sing carnival when the mind freezes
Then turns on its own meat, carnival
Before the long fast, carnival that we turn
To drink at the blood wells of memory.

Savage simplicity, in the bleached palms
Of the self-regarding dancers;
Savage and clear, the energy
Of the self-disclosing dancers.

The flare of a star multiplies
In the Easter sky; each blade
In the clearing is hammered to its shadow.
There is a dipping ring of torches
And dancers counter-revolving in a ring.
There is a belching fire at the heart,
The flames wailing over the mad earth
Whirling hosannas to the coming Beast.

Sing carnival indeed, a feast of man —
You who love language and light, sing while you can.

NORA HARKIN REMEMBERS PEADAR O'DONNELL

> *A man in a red shirt*
> *can neither hide nor retreat*
>   Hugh MacDiarmid

The shutters have closed forever on the big windows.
You'll look no more on street nor heaving field
And the sea will have your spirit, the ungovernable sea
That rolls against Bloody Foreland, rolls against Ireland.

It would be like you, when the gate flies open to duck home
On a flying visit, on the run even from death,
To breathe for a last time air of Tír Chonaill,
Before facing seaward, to the next job to be done.

> *I like to think of their indomitable forms,*
> *Connolly, Mellows, Gilmore, Davitt, Tone,*
> *Standing like stars on the waves, savouring the joke*
> *That indeed they live forever, as you will live forever.*

Perhaps a fisherman far out from home will see the light —
A deckhand out of Burtonport, a kinsman — as your stocky
form
Comes marching out from shore, glowing already in the web
Of new life, looking for comrades and for work.

I'll bet you he keeps his mouth shut, sensible man.
He'll turn from the forepeak, stub out the cigarette
And join in the hauling of the heavy net. His is a world of
work
Like yours, a world of sober fact, of bread and basics.

But his mind is filled with the sea rolling against Ireland,
The ungovernable sea, rolling against Ireland.

Home with the dawn and turning in the door I see him go
To the big windows, flinging the shutters open to the clear air
Before he goes through to wake his wife and daughter,
Humming an air thoughtfully, *O'Donnell Abú.*

THE WITNESS

Lorca chanting a ragged song
In the café of the sad guitars.
By his feet on the stone floor
An almost-empty bottle, by his hand
A candle, cone of light in dark.
The song is choking on itself and silence.

Chairs on the table, a lone waiter
Waters a rich profusion of plants.
Death sits by the door to the street,
Eyes closed, tenderly nursing the song.
I am the stranger buried in the shadows,
Easing my bones on a hard, wooden bench.

I write on a postcard that nothing has been gained here.
The song will not carry him beyond himself,
Will not dissolve the sweating walls,
Cannot unveil the starry dimensions ...

The waiter inhales the invigorated earth.
The courtly old man opens my door home.

Gaia

She torches to touch us, tortured,
Turning slowly on her long axis,
Bones kindling to the dry fire.

Betrayed, seared to the quick,
Deep in herself she nurtures
A dark spring beneath high breasts

And I feel tears
Branding a delta on my cheek,
Issue of that deep spring.

Who would have chosen to live in these times,
On a planet ringed with fire,
The flood welling in her heart that will engulf us?

for John and Evelyn

I father the holocausts like a bull,
I am the yellow flame scouring the womb,
I drink the protein of the bloodflow,
I am the taste of copper and despair.

I am the endless grinding convoys
And the entrails gorged with nations,
Soundlessly bellowing over the endless waves
Of entire nations stampeded to the pit.

My fire is your quickening into death.
I have thickened the humus with blood,
Sifted your fields with bonemeal,
Not a blade of grass but is stained with my work.

Under the grains and orchards,
Under the Autobahns and railroads,
I am the subsoil of black ash
Under the Cities and Cathedrals of the plain.

Mine are the ovens whose smoke hangs
In the chambers of your mind,
In the Zyklon chambers I am the mind
Delighting in its dance of veils.

And I am the silence ticking beneath your pulse
I am the weariness of the daily horrors
Endlessly repeated, I am the numbness and the silence
After the bombers have gone over.

Mine are the children and the burning homes
Mine are the smooth urbanities of Ministers

Mine are the fountains of earth flesh and fire
Mine are the flowers of napalm in the silence.

      I give you a mirror of your own devising
      That you may see me, the god over your shoulder:

Here are the factories and houses,
Here the white hospitals and churches
Here the eternal towers of Auschwitz
Seen in a glass darkly,

Seen in the quiet streets of Dresden
Fused in the vortex of my fire,
The sign you have raised across the living earth
In tribute to my paternal lust and care.

LEAR GARLANDED WITH AGE

Nothing will come of nothing —
The king dripped spittle into
A widening, an appalled silence.
The feathered reptile flashed in the dark,
Fledged in the old man's gut.

Oh he was fastidious in his exile,
His bowels churning, his head in a fever,
Mad in his journeying, yet cleaner in this
Than his crushed and cold companions.

What cracked him open to the wind's work?
His daughter's exile was cliff without shelter.
Here he held court with himself, crying to God
For a straw of meaning, relief from the upland wind.
The Fool and the Blind Man guarded him there.

From where but from death in life, from
Where but from nothing should he climb down,
The long grasses around him like his years
To find at the pit's edge, stopped,
His loving, now his lost, Cordelia?

His eyes in their uneven orbits leap
Across time, grey bloodsoaked arena,
Eyes of a victim, mute.
An old mudcaked father, half a man
Bringing flowers of ruin to a daughter's triumph.

for Seán Lucy

NIGHT LETTER

Whether that gnaws at me which long habit
Persuades me I daily see, or that which
I sometimes, unbearably, touch
And think I know but fail to name,
Dear friend I cannot say.

Night after night I sit here and it gnaws at me,
Something undone that cries out to be done;
It is a dilute acid in my blood,
It is the characters of your name
Tried on a white sheet here before me.

There is an order I can't touch, it sears me.
There is the hollow in my palm, however hard
I push I cannot flatten it to the table.
There is an endless terror in such fact.
I want the order to protect me.

I want the fact of flat to be my guardian —
I skate above electrons when I walk,
I nest among electrons when I sleep —
There are nights here when my floor is a sheet of glass,
The flat face of an endless shaft of darkness.
Tonight again I sweat the darkness out;
An old, broken General in the asylum
I drill my talismans across the table,
Hoping by perseverance and cold patience
To stumble on order that will stop the rout.

Tomorrow again the descent into the city
Down long hills, past old sandstone walls,
Past butcher and breadshop, restaurant and bar —
Calling each thing familiar as a charm,
Hoping to hear the name of what we are.

LONG VALLEY VIGNETTE

In the drained glass,
In the barman's smile as you
Slowly grow absent

As in mirrors that repeat
A childhood nightmare,
No reflection.

You say, we live in Babel.
You say, we live in Hell.
Nobody disagrees.

You stare in the mirror
And childhood is very near,
A thirsted-for oblivion.

Humphrey! Allow me to
Buy this man a drink.

for Humphrey and Rita

YOUR CHILDHOOD

Today, walking in hard light,
Broken, refracted, cascading
Over children at play,
I saw as from high over earth
Your child's face reflecting the light
From the underside of leaves.

There was dust on your cheek my love,
Dust on your burning cheek.

TWIN

I am a voice in towering stillness
I am the absence of that voice
And the child's coat it trails behind closed doors.
I am the memory you will never have,
Incident at the centre of your life.

I am the echo launched both ways at once,
Backward into the blue sea and forward
Into the arms of living death.
I am that death whose cry ripped out the echo,
Mine was the third voice of your conception.

When you first pulsed into a clot of flesh
Beating outward to the rosepink light,
I was the living measure of your need.
When the blue mesh built out beneath your skin,
Humming with blood and sugars,
I was the chord that sang you into life.

When you began the long, bloody slide
Into the lights and airs of this crazed planet,
I was the absence you already felt.
I was the echo fading in your wake,
I was the strongest contraction and the push,
The cry beating against you like white light.

I am the voice you search for and forget,
I am its absence for good reason,
Better to hunt for than to find —
Look in your father's and your mother's grave —
You die if you find me, die if you do not search.

THE THAW
Moscow 1987

A great dome of frost hangs over the taiga,
Blue as the dome of the great mosque of Samarkand.
A great dome of absolute, virgin silence
Pierced by the bell-like voices of unseasonal birds.

The very sap rising in the birches is frost,
The snow underfoot rings with tiny, clear echoes
As the foot of a man crushes whole cities
Of galleried, honeycombed crystal with each step.

Somewhere a simple man is burning logs,
It is mid-morning and time for a cup of tea.
He fancies he hears, dying away through the forest,
The echoes of his axe, notes from a fading bell.

In the honeycomb of his memories, a lone voice is ringing,
Tiny and clear and golden, calling the faithful to prayer.
Meanwhile, over the immense taiga, Mandelstam is trudging
— towards Voronezh, or Moscow?

I was the gesture when you crossed yourself,
The tendon tightening when you arched your foot,
The last bar on the violin, your cue; I was
The swell of woodwind when you crossed the bar,
Who but I had the set so carefully dressed?

I was the dusty board on which you stood
The pod of air beneath your arch, the dust
That filmed your calves, the glint of talc;
I was the sweat in beads at tip of eyebrow,
I was the heat of you moving in the hush.

I was the blaze of light in which you walked,
The cool hand that dimmed the ticking spot,
I was the fly-bar and the drop,
Your grip as you found the pace,
The cage of breath and gesture that you made.

Where is your lover now that you've stepped out
Beyond the daily confines of the self?
The knees that kneel here rested behind his
But the heart, ah the heart stutters to another beat,
The struggle behind your speech

Begins complicity, a foot set treacherously on a bridge.
I am the pole at either end of the bridge.
Mine are the author's fears and yours,
I the possession you both court and fear.
Have I not laid these heads beneath your feet?

I had the image made that lured them in,
I had the food contrived to tempt you,

I am the food of breath, the breath that feeds you
Over the footlights into the cage your compact makes,
I am the darkness when the circuit breaks.

I am the actress and the act,
I am an exquisite gesture and its vanity.
I am the face resumed before the mirror.
I am the unreal street when you step out —
Who but I had the set so carefully dressed?

ELUSIVE

My love she stitched a net of light
And set it up before my path,
At its heart, as black as night,
A carved, curving salmon sat.

Between the apple and the oak
She stopped me on my morning walk
With such an humorous, desperate art
She made me stumble in my talk.

The voice inside me since my birth
Curved off into the shining trees,
My new attention perched there too
And wondered what to make of me.

A blackbird in a bead of light
Trembled on the nearest leaf
And, from behind, his piercing song
Stalked my sudden grief.

A cold wind made the salmon dance
And the same wind brought me down,
From a great height over earth and time
I stood on common ground.

The blackbird spread to the rising wind,
The salmon danced in the net —
Although my love cannot be found
She may come to me yet.

WAKING

Halfway from sleep
Attention snags
On a windwave breasting alders,
Then whirls away on the pollen spume.

I wake in a valley of braided rivers.
Walking through beaded grass,
My whistling loops with the swift
In the smell of broad earth.

Sun ray lances from behind my shoulder,
Crashes against your window in a green spray.

Here are pale mushrooms in a basket,
Cider and fruit, crisp in the frost,
For our breakfast on the mountain. Step
Out and walk with me in the fresh light of day.

RETURN

I can't see my hand at arm's length
But I see her face, shining with mist & sweat
As the boat dances in to the beach.

Nearly dawn: not long now until feet
Slap in the shallows, where water and sand
Have an always shifting frontier.

The creak of the oarlocks is louder, nearer —
Here come the herring gulls, her escort.

THERMAL

Brown hawk spiralling
Over moorland well,
Lower and lower to mate
With his reflection.

Had not the wild rose
Burst into flame
He was lost forever
To the high plain.

SPEAKING TO MY FATHER

How should I now call up that man my father,
Who year after weary year went off to work,
Buried his heart beneath a weight of duty,
Buried himself early so that we might live?

How should I sit here and explain to his shade
That, yes, this is the work I do you died for,
This is the use I make of all that sacrifice,
I move the words as you moved heavy tyres.

True, there is no sickening stench of rubber,
No heat from the curing pans, no rage
At management, choked back by need as much as pride —
But father, the range of uselessness is wide.

Often, as I grew slowly, you'd let slip
A word, a helpless gesture or a look
That shook me to the roots, I'd sense the void
You stubbornly, heroically sweated back.

Now I have everything you lacked, above all
Freedom to shape the workload for the day —
It sounds like freedom, doesn't it? The truth is,
I hate the shiftwork just as much as you did.

There are days lately, as I thicken in years,
When I feel your sinews shift inside my frame,
I catch a look of yours in the mirror, shaving:
Mild, ironical, weary, a bit resigned —

But something else, too: your athlete's way
Of planting the feet carefully when troubled,

72

Shoulder square to the blow that may come,
Hands tense to defend what you hold dear.

What troubled you most? The question shies away
When I stab with my pen, clumsy as ever
— I don't even rightly know what troubles me,
Ignorant as when I rode upon your knee.

What would you make of me, I wonder, sitting here
Long after midnight, searching for the words to
Bring you back, soliciting the comfort of your shade
For the odd, useless creature that you made?

Here is the end of all that education,
The void is as close to me as it ever was to you,
I make poems of love as you and Rose made children,
Blindly, in hope and trust, because I must.

Father, comrade, the same anger with the world
But not your patience moves me; I make you this,
A toy in words to re-introduce myself
And to ask, what must I do to be your child again?

RIMBAUD'S NURSE

I am the nurse of the small hours,
Crushing phials of morphine with my heel,
I am the oiled linoleum angel,
The rack in my look and the cold bedframe.

In the case of Arthur Rimbaud ...
In the Hospital of the Immaculate Conception
Marseilles 1891,
Where his knee burned to bend again
And the crows of Cyprus creaked in his eyes,
Where his leg was and was not,
Where his wrist burned with an old wound,
A wound of love that was not, neither wound nor love,
Over and over I listened to him beg
Let me go to the sea, let me go to the sea.

I was the swarming cancer of his need,
Black Venus hull-down on the horizon.

I am the starch and press of night
I am the sweat pressed from nightmare
I am the nurse of the small hours
Crushing phials of morphine with my heel.

For pity I reserve a particular silence
Neither memory nor oblivion in my gift.

THE PROMISED GARDEN

There is a garden where our hearts converse,
At ease beside clear water, dreaming
A whole and perfect future for yourself,
Myself, our children and our friends.

And if we must rise and leave,
Put on identity and fight,
Each day more desperate than the last
And further from our future, that
Is no more than honour and respect shown
To all blocked from the garden that we own.

There is a garden at the heart of things,
Our oldest memory guards it with her strong will.
Those who by love and work attain there
Bathe in her living waters, lift up their hearts and
Turn again to share the steep privations of the hill;
They walk in the market but their feet are still.

There is a garden where our hearts converse,
At ease beside clear water, dreaming
A whole and perfect future for yourself,
Myself, our children and our friends.

for Suzanne

KHAYAAM WAS RIGHT

Khayaam was right, we are toys
On the table of existence, but cast
Beyond the nursery tale's confines,
You to your unknown future, I to mine.

Prison me in your dreams of what should be,
Set me to match a long-prefigured step,
What do you have then if you hold me
But a child's toy to guard in sleep?

Gently, the tales of childhood are no more,
The nursery beams are charred, they stink in the rain,
And we must make new mysteries of our own
Before we achieve that innocence again.

Gently, the road behind us falls away,
The walled garden fades into a dream.
Kiss me and touch my cheek, then choose your path:
Neither will keep this rendezvous again.